The Urbana Free Library

To renew: call 217-367-4057
or go to *urbanafreelibrary.org*
and select "My Account"

CAUSE AND EFFECT: The Bill of Rights

The First Amendment:
Freedom of Speech and Religion

BY JOHN MICKLOS, JR.

Consultant:
Richard Bell, PhD
Associate Professor of History
University of Maryland, College Park

CAPSTONE PRESS
a capstone imprint

Fact Finders Books are published by Capstone Press,
1710 Roe Crest Drive, North Mankato, Minnesota 56003
www.mycapstone.com

Library of Congress Cataloging-in-Publication Data
Names: Micklos, John, author.
Title: The First Amendment : freedom of speech and religion / by John
    Micklos, Jr.
Description: North Mankato, Minnesota : Capstone Press, 2018. | Series: Fact
    finders. Cause and effect: the Bill of Rights | Includes bibliographical
    references and index.
Identifiers: LCCN 2017006677
ISBN 978-1-5157-7164-7 (library binding)
ISBN 978-1-5157-7177-7 (paperback)
ISBN 978-1-5157-7182-1 (eBook PDF)
Subjects: LCSH: Freedom of speech—United States—Juvenile literature. |
    United States. Constitution. 1st Amendment—Juvenile literature. | Freedom
    of religion—United States—Juvenile literature. | Freedom of the
    press—United States—Juvenile literature.
Classification: LCC KF4770 .M53 2018 | DDC 342.7308/52—dc23
LC record available at https://lccn.loc.gov/2017006677

Editorial Credits
Brenda Haugen, editor; Brent Slingsby, designer; Tracey Engel, media researcher;
Katy LaVigne,, production specialist

Source Notes
Page 10, sidebar, line 5: K.M. Kostyal. *Founding Fathers: The Fight for Freedom and the Birth of American Liberty.*
Washington, D.C.: National Geographic, 2014, p. 62.

Photo Credits
Getty Images: Bettmann, 11, Cultura RM Exclusive/Frank and Helena, cover, Popperfoto, 25; iStockphoto:
duncan1890, 16, rrodrickbeiler, 20; Library of Congress: LC-DIG-pga-03325, 17, LC-DIG-pga-07513, 26, World Journal
Tribune photo by Ira Rosenberg, cph.3c15435, 19; North Wind Picture Archives: 9, 12, 13, 14, 27; Shutterstock:
Christopher Penler, 29, Everett Historical, 24, J Main, 18, Joseph Gruber, 5, Tischenko Irina, 7, cover design element,
Tupungato, 22; Wikimedia: US Government, 23
Design Elements: Shutterstock

Printed and bound in the USA.
010399F17

Table of *Contents*

Creating a
BILL OF RIGHTS

People in the United States have many freedoms. Among them is the freedom of speech. Americans can say whatever is on their minds. They also can worship — or choose not to worship — however they wish. The government does not **censor** what people read. It also allows a free flow of ideas on television and on the Internet. In addition, people can gather peacefully wherever they want. And if they have concerns, they can **petition** the government and ask for the issues to be addressed.

Most Americans take these freedoms for granted. The founders of the United States did not. Under British rule, American colonists were not promised these freedoms.

censor—to remove material considered morally or politically offensive or harmful
petition—present a formal written request
Constitution—legal document that describes the basic form of the U.S. government and the rights of citizens
amendment—an addition or change

4

American leaders wrote the **Constitution** in 1787, four years after the treaty ending the Revolutionary War (1775–1783). The Constitution described how the new nation should be run. But some people feared the new government might grow too strong. They worried that government leaders might limit their freedoms as Britain had done. The founders listened to these fears. They added a Bill of Rights to the new Constitution in 1789. The Bill of Rights included 10 **amendments**. The amendments outlined certain key freedoms. The government cannot take away these rights without changing the Constitution.

People gathered to protest shootings involving police in 2016.

The First
AMENDMENT

The Bill of Rights spells out freedoms for individuals and states. The nation's founders **debated** what these key freedoms should be. One says that people are free to worship as they wish. Others allow them to speak freely and gather peacefully. People also have the right to petition the government if they have concerns. These rights are listed in the First Amendment.

The beginning of the First Amendment is called the Establishment Clause. It prevents Congress from establishing a national religion. The rest of the amendment is called the Exercise Clause. It outlines rights that citizens are free to exercise, or use.

FAST FACT:

The First Amendment wasn't always first. The founders originally drafted 12 amendments in the Bill of Rights. This amendment moved up when states failed to **ratify** the first two amendments in the Bill of Rights. One of the amendments that failed dealt with setting the number of representatives in Congress. The other dealt with pay for senators and representatives.

debate—discuss, looking at the arguments on both sides
ratify—formally approve

The Bill of Rights

Amendment I

Congress shall make no law respecting an establishment of religion, or prohibiting the free exercise thereof; or abridging the freedom of speech, or of the press; or the right of the people peaceably to assemble, and to petition the government for a redress of grievances.

Amendment II

A well regulated militia, being necessary to the security of a free state, the right of the people to keep and bear arms, shall not be infringed.

Amendment III

No soldier shall, in time of peace be quartered in any house, without the consent of the owner, nor in time of war, but in a manner to be prescribed by law.

Amendment IV

The right of the people to be secure in their persons, houses, papers, and effects, against unreasonable searches and seizures, shall not be violated, and no warrants shall issue, but upon probable cause, supported by oath or affirmation, and particularly describing the place to be searched, and the persons or things to be seized.

Amendment V

No person shall be held to answer for a capital, or otherwise infamous crime, unless on a presentment or indictment of a grand jury, except in cases arising in the land or naval forces, or in the militia, when in actual service in time of war or public danger; nor shall any person be subject for the same offense to be twice put in jeopardy of life or limb; nor shall be compelled in any criminal case to be a witness against himself, nor be deprived of life, liberty, or property, without due process of law; nor shall private property be taken for public use, without just compensation.

Amendment VI

In all criminal prosecutions, the accused shall enjoy the right to a speedy and public trial, by an impartial jury of the state and district wherein the crime shall have been committed, which district shall have been previously ascertained by law, and to be informed of the nature and cause of the accusation; to be confronted with the witnesses against him; to have compulsory process for obtaining witnesses in his favor, and to have the assistance of counsel for his defense.

Amendment VII

In suits at common law, where the value in controversy shall exceed twenty dollars, the right of trial by jury shall be preserved, and no fact tried by a jury, shall be otherwise reexamined in any court of the United States, than according to the rules of the common law.

Amendment VIII

Excessive bail shall not be required, nor excessive fines imposed, nor cruel and unusual punishments inflicted.

Amendment IX

The enumeration in the Constitution, of certain rights, shall not be construed to deny or disparage others retained by the people.

Amendment X

The powers not delegated to the United States by the Constitution, nor prohibited by it to the states, are reserved to the states respectively, or to the people.

Causes of the
FIRST AMENDMENT

Why is the First Amendment so important? It outlines people's most basic rights. It talks about major freedoms colonists didn't have during British rule.

Cause #1: People Wanted Freedom to Worship as They Chose

Religion comes at the beginning of the First Amendment for a reason. In the 1600s and 1700s, many people across Europe were **persecuted** because of their religious beliefs. Many came to the colonies so they could worship freely.

Religious freedom varied among colonies. Rhode Island and Pennsylvania welcomed people of all beliefs. Some colonies did not. For example, Massachusetts forced Roger Williams to leave the colony in 1635. Why? His religious beliefs differed from the colony's leaders. Williams dared to speak his mind. As punishment, he was **banished**. The next year Williams founded the colony of Rhode Island. He made sure religious freedom was allowed there.

Pennsylvania was formed as a colony for people seeking religious freedom. The colony's founder, William Penn, had been jailed in England for his **Quaker** beliefs. He called the colony's approach to religion a "Holy Experiment."

persecute—to punish or treat badly for one's beliefs
banished—forced to leave a place against one's will
Quaker—a member of the Religious Society of Friends, a group founded in the 1600s, who attends silent religious services without a preacher and opposes war

Cause #2: Freedom of Speech Was Limited

In many European countries in the 1600s and 1700s, people could not speak freely. They could not criticize the government. That's another reason people came to the **New World**.

But freedom of speech was limited even in the colonies. People could be jailed for criticizing the king of England or speaking in favor of independence. The British viewed this as **treason**. Citizens of the United States wanted to make sure the new government never had the power to limit free speech.

FAST FACT:

Virginia legislator Patrick Henry called for the colonies to seek independence in 1775. He knew the British could charge him with treason for such talk, but he continued to speak his mind. "I know not what course others may take; but, as for me, give me liberty or give me death!" he said.

New World—the name given to the Americas as they were being explored and settled
treason—the act of betraying one's country

*Patrick Henry
delivering his famous
speech in 1775*

Standing Up for the Truth

Printer Peter Zenger published letters criticizing the governor of New York in 1733 and 1734. A warrant for his arrest was issued in November 1734. He was charged with **libel**. After spending nearly a year in jail, Zenger's trial began August 4, 1735. His lawyer argued that if what Zenger printed was true, it wasn't libel. The jury found Zenger not guilty. Even today people may criticize others in print if the criticisms are true.

Cause #3: Citizens Believed a Strong Press Would Keep Government in Check

Any printed criticism of the king or British **authority** was called libel under British rule. People who printed such criticisms could be fined or jailed. They might even be accused of treason. Treason could be punished by death. Still, some colonists refused to be silenced. Benjamin Franklin and Thomas Paine published material that could be considered treasonous.

Citizens of the new United States wanted newspapers to be free to criticize the government and its leaders. They believed this would help keep the government from becoming too powerful.

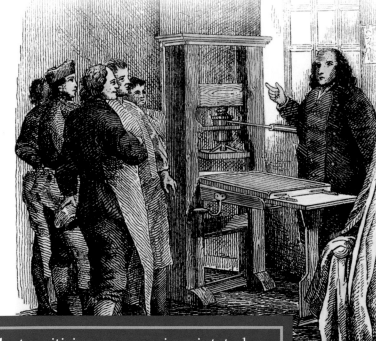

Benjamin Franklin (right) had his own printing press.

libel—to criticize someone in print; today it means printing criticism that is false
authority—having power over someone

Cause #4: Citizens Wanted to Gather Peacefully to Discuss Issues

Imagine if the government kept you from meeting your friends in public. The freedom for groups to meet publicly was not guaranteed under British rule. The British often broke up gatherings of colonists. They feared the colonists might be plotting independence. It didn't even matter if the people gathered peacefully.

Colonists met to discuss how the British were treating them.

Freedom of assembly helped make sure the government didn't grow too powerful. In those days, people did not have television, phones, and the Internet. They discussed issues in person. They met in town halls, taverns, and private homes. The nation's founders knew many citizens did not want to limit such meetings. These citizens wanted people to feel free to gather and discuss issues and concerns.

Threatening the Freedom to Assemble

New York's governing body, called the assembly, tried to take a stand in 1765. It refused to cooperate with Britain's Quartering Act. The act required the colonies to provide housing, called quarters, for British soldiers stationed there. Sometimes this meant housing soldiers in private homes. Britain said the assembly could not conduct business unless it agreed to pay for housing the soldiers. Faced with this threat, the assembly agreed to Britain's Quartering Act.

Cause #5: A Need for Government to Listen to Concerns

The right to petition the government about concerns dates back to 1215. King John of England agreed to give this and other rights to rich landowners. England did not give this right to the colonies. Many times before the Revolutionary War, colonial leaders tried to petition the British government. They wanted to express their concerns. Each time the British refused to address the issues.

Citizens wanted to make sure the new U.S. government would listen if they had concerns. That is why the nation's founders included the clause about petitioning the government.

King John (seated in tall chair) led England from 1199 until his death in 1216.

Colonial leaders sent the Olive Branch Petition to England in July 1775. They listed their concerns. King George III refused to consider the petition. This led the colonies to break away from England.

Effects of the
FIRST AMENDMENT

Citizens in the late 1700s saw the First Amendment as vital. It protected some of their most basic rights. It continues to have important effects on people's lives today.

Effect #1: Government Does Not Promote Religion

The founders of the United States thought religious freedom was critical to a healthy country. The First Amendment stated that Congress can never establish a national religion. People may worship however they wish.

Over time, **Supreme Court** rulings have led to the removal of anything that promotes religion in public schools, government offices, and public buildings. Bible readings and prayer were also stopped in public schools. Displays of the **Ten Commandments** have been removed as well.

The U.S. Supreme Court Building is in Washington, D.C.

Fighting for Freedom of Worship

Heavyweight boxing champion Muhammad Ali refused to serve in the U.S. Army in 1967. He said being forced to fight in a war would go against his beliefs as a Muslim. He said that would take away his freedom to practice his religion. Ali was stripped of his heavyweight title. Two and a half years later, the U.S. Supreme Court ruled in Ali's favor.

Supreme Court—the highest court in the United States

Ten Commandments—a set of 10 rules that are key in the religions of Judaism and Christianity

Effect #2: People Can Speak Freely

The freedom to freely express one's views is among the most basic freedoms. People in the United States are free to criticize the government. They can say things that other people might disagree with. The United States offers greater freedom of speech than most countries.

draft—a system of recruiting soldiers into military service
conviction—finding someone guilty of a crime

Protesters often gather in Washington, D.C., to get the attention of lawmakers.

Free speech does have limits. People can't share information that would put the nation at risk. That happens most often during wars. During World War I (1914–1918), Congress passed a law against saying things that might keep people from serving in the Army. A man was jailed for passing out flyers against the **draft**. The Supreme Court upheld the **conviction**. Justice Oliver Wendell Holmes said the government could limit free speech if the words "create a clear and present danger."

These policies changed over the years. By the 1960s, the government and the courts allowed people to protest the Vietnam War (1954–1975). In 1969 the Supreme Court ruled that even burning a U.S. flag in protest is protected as freedom of expression. Today the right to protest against war — or almost anything — is respected, as long as the protest is peaceful.

Students and Freedom of Speech

Some free speech issues relate directly to students. The U.S. Supreme Court's ruling in *Board of Education v. Pico* (1982) stated that school officials may not remove books from school libraries simply because they disagree with the ideas contained in them. The ruling in *Tinker v. Des Moines Independent Community School District* (1969) allowed students to wear black armbands at school to protest the Vietnam War.

Cause #3: The Government Guarantees Freedom of the Press

Freedom of the press was a key point for many U.S. citizens. When the Bill of Rights was written, the press included newspapers, pamphlets, and books. Today the press also includes television, radio, and the Internet.

Freedom of the press allows people to publish almost anything. This includes criticism of the government. To be protected against a charge of libel, the writer or publisher must make sure the information is true. When writing about a public figure, the protection against libel is even broader. The author just needs to make sure the statement, even if it proves not to be true, is not made with **malice**.

Freedom of the press does not cover **obscene** material. A Supreme Court ruling defined what is obscene. Obscene material is offensive and lacks serious value.

Freedom of the press has been one of the country's most precious rights since the United States was founded.

The Sedition Act

The United States took a step back from freedom of the press in 1798. That year Congress passed the **Sedition** Act. The act made it against the law to print any criticism of the government. People who did could be fined and face up to two years in jail. Public outrage doomed the new law. It lasted only three years.

malice—desire to cause pain or distress
obscene—not meeting normal standards of decency
sedition—speech or writing that tries to bring rebellion against authority

Effect #4: People Can Gather Peaceably

Colonists were not allowed to gather peacefully to protest against British rule. Therefore, citizens of the new United States placed great value on this freedom. Over the years freedom of assembly has played an important role in some major U.S. movements.

Thousands of women marched on Washington, D.C., in 1913. They demanded the right to vote. Their protests and marches continued for several more years. Their efforts paid off. In 1920 the 19th Amendment to the Constitution allowed women to vote.

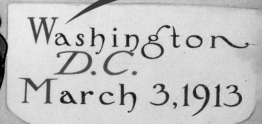

the cover of the program for the National American Women's Suffrage Association march

Marches and peaceful protests also played a key role in the civil rights movement of the 1960s. Hundreds of thousands of people gathered in Washington, D.C., in 1963. They sought equal rights for African-Americans. People listened as the Reverend Martin Luther King Jr. gave his famous I Have a Dream speech. A year later the Civil Rights Act of 1964 passed. The new law guaranteed equal treatment for all people.

Protest Turns Tragic

National Guardsmen shot and killed four unarmed students at Kent State University in Ohio on May 4, 1970. The students were protesting the Vietnam War. The shooting sent shockwaves throughout the nation. It went against the First Amendment right of peaceful assembly. The shooting led to protests across the country. These protests continued until the United States began to withdraw its soldiers from Vietnam.

Effect #5: People Can Petition the Government About Concerns

What do you do if you have a concern to share with the government? The Bill of Rights gives you the right to file a petition. In the petition you can state your concerns.

However, government leaders do not act on all petitions they receive. Even if they do act, they might not take the action the petitioner wanted. In the 1830s the Cherokee nation petitioned the U.S. Senate. They asked to be able to stay on their tribal land. The Senate did not act on the Cherokees' plea. In 1838 the Cherokees were forced to leave their homeland.

John Ross was the main chief of the Cherokees from 1828 until 1866.

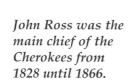

FAST FACT:

Today, the Internet makes it easy to petition the government. The White House website tells you how to do it.

THE CASE

OF

THE CHEROKEE NATION

against

THF STATE OF GEORGIA:

ARGUED AND DETERMINED AT

THE SUPREME COURT OF THE UNITED STATES,

JANUARY TERM 1831.

WITH

AN APPENDIX,

Containing the Opinion of Chancellor Kent on the Case ; the Treaties between the United States and the Cherokee Indians ; the Act of Congress of 1802, entitled ' An Act to regulate intercourse with the Indian tribes, &c.'; and the Laws of Georgia relative to the country occupied by the Cherokee Indians, within the boundary of that State.

BY RICHARD PETERS,

COUNSELLOR AT LAW.

Philadelphia:
JOHN GRIGG, 9 NORTH FOURTH STREET.
1831.

part of the Supreme Court record in the Cherokees' case

The First Amendment
TODAY

On September 11, 2001, terrorists struck the World Trade Center in New York City. They also struck the Pentagon in Arlington, Virginia. Those attacks jolted the nation's sense of safety. They also led to new policies regarding freedom of speech.

Soon after the attacks, Congress passed the Patriot Act. The law lessened some types of personal freedom. The goal was to prevent further terrorist attacks. Section 215 allowed the government to check the phone usage of suspected **radicals**. It also allowed the government to see what they borrowed from their local libraries or viewed online. The people did not even know their records were being checked.

Some people believe the Patriot Act helps prevent terrorist acts. After all, some Internet sites show how to build homemade bombs. Shouldn't the government have the right to monitor suspicious people who seek out such information? And should the First Amendment protect people who post such material?

Other people believe the Patriot Act goes too far. When the government monitors people it thinks might be terrorists, it may often be monitoring innocent people as well. Doesn't this violate their First Amendment rights? Also, Muslims are often targeted for monitoring because radical Muslims have been involved in terror attacks. But most Muslims are not terrorists. How can their religious freedom be protected? These are difficult questions, and the answers are not always clear.

People continue to debate these First Amendment issues today. These discussions will help the nation balance the rights of individuals with the need to keep people safe.

FAST FACT:

Protesters marched in several American cities following the 2016 presidential election. Some people claimed the protests were anti-American. Others said the protests provided a perfect example of democracy in action. The First Amendment guarantees the right to protest. It also guarantees the right to express one's opinion — pro or con — about the protest.

radical—someone who has extreme political or social views

GLOSSARY

amendment (uh-MEND-muhnt)—an addition or change

authority (uh-THAW-ruh-tee)—having power over someone

banished (BAN-isht)—forced to leave a place against one's will

censor (SEN-suhr)—to remove material considered morally or politically offensive or harmful

Constitution (kahn-stuh-TOO-shuhn)—legal document that describes the basic form of the U.S. government and the rights of citizens

conviction (kuhn-VIK-shuhn)—finding someone guilty of a crime

debate (di-BAYT)—discuss, looking at the arguments on both sides

draft (DRAFT)—a system of recruiting soldiers into military service

libel (LYE-buhl)—to criticize someone in print; today it means printing criticism that is false

malice (MAL-iss)—desire to cause pain or distress

New World (NOO WURLD)—the name given to the Americas as they were being explored and settled

obscene (ahb-SEEN)—not meeting normal standards of decency

persecute (PUR-suh-kyoot)—to punish or treat badly for one's beliefs

petition (puh-TISH-uhn)—present a formal written request

Quaker (KWAY-kur)—a member of the Religious Society of Friends, a group founded in the 1600s, who attends silent religious services without a preacher and opposes war

radical (RAH-duh-kuhl)—someone who has extreme political or social views

ratify (RAH-tuh-fye)—formally approve

sedition (SUH-di-shuhn)—speech or writing that tries to bring rebellion against authority

Supreme Court (suh-PREEM KORT)—the highest court in the United States

Ten Commandments (TEN kuh-MAND-muhnts)—a set of 10 rules that are key in the religions of Judaism and Christianity

treason (TREE-zuhn)—the act of betraying one's country

READ MORE

Baxter, Roberta. *The Bill of Rights*. Chicago: Heinemann Library, 2013.

Krensky, Stephen. *The Bill of Rights*. Tarrytown, New York: Marshall Cavendish, 2012.

Krull, Kathleen. *A Kid's Guide to America's Bill of Rights*. New York: Harper, 2015.

Spier, Peter. *We the People: The Constitution of the United States*. New York: Doubleday, 2014.

INTERNET SITES

Use FactHound to find Internet sites related to this book.

Visit *www.facthound.com*

Just type in 9781515771647 and go.

 Check out projects, games and lots more at
www.capstonekids.com

CRITICAL THINKING QUESTIONS

1. Why were citizens of the new United States so interested in a Bill of Rights that spelled out key freedoms? How might the nation's development have been different if there had not been any Bill of Rights?

2. Why was freedom of religion the first thing mentioned in the First Amendment?

3. What information in the chapter titled "The First Amendment Today" helps you see that there are varying points of view regarding the lessening of personal freedoms in an attempt to prevent terrorism?

INDEX